YOU CAN'T SAVE ME FROM MYSELF

NICOLE BRITTNEY

ISBN: 978-1-7377891-0-9 (Paperback)
ISBN: 978-1-7377891-1-6 (Epub)

Any references to historical events, real people, or real places are used fictitiously. Names, characters, and places are products of the author's imagination.

First printing edition 2021.

Uncovering Your Power Publishing
Laurel, MD 20707

www.uncoveringyourpower.com

And then I realized...my journey to peace and self actualization had little to do with the world around me and everything to do with ME.

TABLE OF CONTENTS

AUTHOR'S NOTE

So many of us are walking this earth, searching for the keys to life…

We look up YouTube videos, self-help books, the next best blog or magazine article, all in an attempt to uncover a sign to help us better understand our journey through someone else's eyes.

Life is a cycle.

The uniqueness of this journey can't be defined from another's perspective. While we can gather wisdom and guidance from others, ultimately, conquering this journey will take action from us as individuals.

Our mindsets, our actions and our attitudes are for us to determine. Everything that we receive or fail to receive in this lifetime is within our grasp.

I suffered and wandered in confusion for so long only to realize that my journey to peace and self actualization had little to do with the world around me and everything to do with ME.

Once you realize the true power within yourself, you will see that each trial, tribulation and obstacle at hand will be overcome with very similar approaches. You will begin to realize the secrets and hidden gems within your journey, and that no hardship was so much a hardship but a path to your own self-discovery.

Through sharing my own personal milestones and meaningful stories of wisdom that have been passed along to me, I will guide you through my journey to self-actualization.

I ask that you not just read this book from a lense of the stories shared, but that you use it to consider similarities and circumstances within your own journey. From there, I challenge you to build a path to delivery for yourself, as I continue to do within my own life.

My hope is that what is offered here provides you with a better understanding of what the ups and downs in your life might be trying to teach you. Perhaps there are stones left unturned in your own walk that you can draw wisdom from through further exploration.

Success, love, peace and empowerment are the birthright of us all. The more that we aim to see the light at the end of our darkness, the more we stand to attain and aspire to as individuals and a community at large.

May peace, love and an open mind guide you through this book and your unique path to a more empowered *you*.

With love,
Nicole Brittney

Part I
DEALING WITH THE PAST

The past shapes our future.

If we cannot learn value from our past experiences, we will find ourselves stagnant in uncovering our true potential.

Ignoring past trauma may *feel* comfortable but it is like reading only the end of a book and trying to speak to how the story played out. You either make it up or gain creativity around what you want it to be.

But our life story is just that, *our life story.*

It is not something we can make up or create a story around.

Internally, we must accept and evaluate it for what it is and was.

We cannot be our full selves until we comfortably address how we got to the mindsets, decisions and attitudes we walk in today.

Dealing with the past takes courage and dedication. It is the foundation to actively defining who we choose to be as people. Life can happen to you, but it's so much more empowering when you can use understanding and perspective to begin to steer your life in the direction you'd like to go, from the driver's seat.

Begin to envision yourself as the creator of your universe.

We were once helpless children but today we take on a new stance - the creators of our own universe.

SELF REFLECTION:

As you read the following stories - consider your journey up to now.

- Do you have an outlet for past pain?
- Are you moving forward with love and true understanding of yourself?
- Are there aspects of your childhood and upbringing that you have not addressed?
- Are there relationships from your past that may not be serving the future you?
- Have you forgiven yourself for what the younger you did not know?

1.

THE STRENGTH OF A WARRIOR

Have you ever had a dream that felt so real you had to convince yourself that it was only a figment of your imagination?...

Not actually real.

Not a premonition…

But just a subconscious thought that felt much deeper than it was in all actuality...

I was running.

It seemed to be a race or event of some sort yet I was the only one taking part.

While the environment didn't seem to indicate that of a race -

The mentality in which I ran proved different.

I was on a mission.

Outside.

Trees, sidewalks, pavement and a mountain somewhere in the distance.

Unaware of my destination but full speed ahead, nonetheless.

I stepped on a board that somehow seemed to get stuck to the bottom of my shoe.

I had no time to stop and take a look.

I had to keep running.

I felt an aching in my foot and knew with each stride that the board remained.

Yet still -

I ran.

Ran until grey skies turned to darkness.

Ran until I could see my stopping point.

Not marked, but a destination I knew to be the end...

I stopped, sat on the edge of a sidewalk, and painfully removed my shoe.

The board was still cemented to my shoe by three long and very deeply puncturing nails.

I could feel the sharp edges of each nail being removed from my flesh, one by one.

I couldn't believe it.

I became angry, expressing my thoughts out loud.

Who would do that?!

Who would leave a board of nails on a running trail?!

The thought made me so mad I could feel the rage in my subconsciously sleeping body.

People knew that others would be running along this path yet they left a board of nails lying face up for someone to step on?!

I held my foot in one hand and my shoe in the other with the board of nails now laying by my footstep.

Somehow, at this point, my foot no longer ached.

This was a sudden realization, though the wounds were still visibly present on my foot...

Mentally, I just wanted to make sense of it all.

I wanted to make sense of something that had no reason.

A dream.

Soon after that, I awoke.

I've found myself at so many crossroads of life wondering, why?

Why was the road I was promised filled with so much debris?

So much heartache?

So much confusion and so much pain...

It seemed so simple of a concept for others to just walk in righteousness.

Treat others how they'd like to be treated.

Love without an agenda.

Clean up behind yourself and leave the world a better place for the person coming behind you.

No matter the season, I was always running into what *seemed* to be somebody else's trash, in the direct path of what was supposed to be *my* clean journey.

I learned with time that in order to get ahead, I had to run *through it.*

Whatever the debris may be, I had to -

Step on it.

Get cut by it.

Get angry and mad about it.

Just to have to gather myself and remember -

To just keep running…

And I'm still running.

Each and every day.

The journey that I thought would be clear, has yet to be.

There are still obstacles -

Still boards of nails and debris.

Cutting through the bottoms of my feet, even deeper with every step.

Yet still,

I run.

I run because my destination is forever moving.

I run because my destination is forever evolving and forever changing.

I can duck and dodge what I see coming! -

But through the fog and grey, there is no way for me to avoid it all.

A destination lies ahead with little time to waste and no real answers for its confusion...

So even when the fresh blisters on my feet stumble upon a new sharp board that breaks the skin and penetrates me to the bloody vein.

I have learned,

through experience -

That this is my cross to bear,

my wounds to heal,

and my head that I must hold high.

The challenges are part of the journey.

And to succeed and conquer,
no matter what -

I must keep running.

2.

REPURPOSE YOUR PAIN

Writing has always been an integral part of my healing process and my ability to have a deeper understanding of myself as a woman.

As a young lady growing up, poetry was my outlet for self expression and discovery. I shared my writings with my girlfriends, in church functions and as my 'talent' for local talent shows and events.

Whether I still (physically) hold the writing or not, the most intimate aspects of my life have been captured with a pen and paper or keyboard and computer.

When I die, my words will continue to speak through me. In writing and capturing my thoughts and self expression, I have created the framework for my legacy. I have outlined my dreams with the beautiful brushstrokes of my fingers and wrists.

I have given my family and future babies a part of Nicole that can never be taken away or forgotten.

My words, like a gift, can be passed down as history, as teachings, as healing and as reflections to the depths of my soul and inner being.

I found that through writing and creativity, my pain could be released and no matter the worldly circumstances, my soul was able to fly again.

I am soaring to new heights and I want to share this gift with anyone willing to receive it.

Pain is just energy, waiting to be freed.

I am afraid that with the structure and mindsets of society today, there will be very few who understand this concept and even fewer who invest in using their pain to fuel the energy they put out into this world, *purposefully*.

We cannot grow to break generational bondage if we don't first mend and heal the damage passed down to us.

How can we heal what is not discussed?

How can we heal what is not acknowledged or given care to?

How can we wipe away tears that we don't allow ourselves to cry?

How can we show someone they can be loved despite faults if we point a finger to shame instead of opening our arms to embrace and encourage change?

The current highlights of everything good, luxurious and flashy reveal more to me around what's not being said, than what is...

I struggled with the worst moments of my life, at many stages of my life, *figuratively* alone.

There are hurting souls in our midst that don't have an outlet for release.

Relationship building and wisdom sharing is of the utmost importance and a presence we need to deliberately encourage and cultivate within our communities.

I choose to see and share my life as God intended. With truth and dignity. With faults, with chaos, with peace and with beauty. Each aspect of my life has seen them all. I can get dressed up and you'd never imagine the path these ten toes have walked upon. I can stand with my chin to the sky while still acknowledging the burdens aching through my limbs.

I don't break under the weight of the world, I endure it.

And I do so in essence to share with you. To share stories of beauty and pain, of triumphs and defeat. Stories of wisdom I wish my mother would have shared with me. Stories embracing the wounds and hugging the little girl my father could not.

My purpose is to show you just how powerful and how loved you really are.

My purpose is to help you uncover your unique footprint on this earth that is so much deeper than your last Instagram or Facebook post.

My purpose is to challenge you.

To challenge your thoughts.

To encourage you to stop going with the flow, just for the heck of it, and to light your own path instead!

My purpose is to inspire you and to reveal the truth - *that you can endure and grow from anything life throws at you, if you just learn to transform it.*

Pain is just energy, waiting to be freed.

Energy that we can transform and do very special things with, if we would only be open to allowing ourselves this right.

Give yourself permission to live, laugh, love and HEAL. And then do it all over again...

3.

GENERATIONAL TRAUMA

I want you to meet my mother.

She was known for her beauty.

Men aspired to be with her. Women aspired to mimic her walk, her demeanor, her style. She was known to stop traffic. She was known to be the talk of the town.

When beauty meets the eye, substance is oftentimes lost and many can't see the depth behind the visual.

My mother never experienced true love until her most recent years.

Yes, she was adored, but *never* was she loved.

From her own mother to the lovers in her life she was a victim of abuse, belittlement and abandonment. Childhood scars hidden behind beautiful eyes and a physique that could entice jealousy, rage and desire.

Secrets behind her glance that onlookers could not fathom.

The love my mother wanted from this life was replaced by others' ability to use, belittle and manipulate her weaknesses. Her desire for love. Her need for security after experiencing abandonment. Her mental limitations. Her desires for a home and the support and nurturing that she needed as a child.

She never really grew up.

Her young mind and its childlike demeanor were a part of her personality. In being as such, she became a woman that people could easily influence. Her spirit seemed to act as a magnet to others' pain and emptiness.

You would be surprised at the urge in some people, the power that they feel when given the ability to tear down and destroy something so beautiful, because of the hatred brewing within themselves.

Beauty without protection is nothing more than a target.

I did not grow up knowing my mother. I did not learn of her story until more recent years but somehow walked in similar footsteps.

During the depths of my path to self healing I had to acknowledge that the demon on my back was bigger than me. It was about a curse that had to be broken. A new path that had to be laid.

In all of my years of chaos, I did not decide to more deliberately change my life, until I better understood my purpose.

It may seem silly, but I didn't choose to invest in healthier relationships solely based on the strength of my own personal well being.

The previously broken me did not have the awareness of self and true love to make that decision.

But I did find the strength to change based on the idea of my legacy.

I decided to change for myself because I knew that the life I was living would not allow me to be an example, or lay the foundation for change, that I was meant to lay for my family and future children.

I had to change because I knew deep down that allowing myself to be belittled in a place of love directly conflicted with my purpose and my strength. It conflicted with my desire to build a life far greater than myself and my own understanding.

It conflicted with my ability to loosen the chains of bondage that others before me could not.

Uncovering my life's purpose saved me.

Time and time again, I thank my mother.

I thank her for all of her many sacrifices.

I thank her for the tears she shed that no one was there to catch.

For the security that no one was there to provide.

For all of the misuse and beatings at the hands of men and women and family members who never loved her.

For experiencing the pain of isolation for choosing to not be beaten another moment.

For being called names and mocked for her weaknesses, instead of being offered the help that she needed to find deliverance.

My mother's pain could have laid the foundation for my defeat. Just as her mother's pain laid the foundation for so many of hers…

My mother's sufferings and lack of knowing were a sacrifice to the self discovery that I was left to find...

Life is nothing more than a cycle. A story that repeats itself, year after year, generation after generation, trauma after trauma.

Breaking that cycle requires dedication, strength and an unwavering commitment.

It takes hope and goodness and love.

It takes forgiveness, understanding and compassion.

When I began to draft *Uncovering Your Power*, I had no intention of doing anything with the writings. A simple google sheet, nothing more than my thoughts in the form of words. My pain being released in another embodiment. My tears dancing to life...

My ability to put action into a new life of loneliness where I did not know anything else to do but to write.

While the story is fictional, the depth behind my feelings and understanding is one of the most real life pieces of art I have ever created.

My ability to be vulnerable and share this piece of art has given me a chance to put into words what so many men and women have experienced in the silence of their hearts:

Organically good people, *frustrated with being used and mistreated.*

Women, searching for love and being hurt because of their desire to embrace and find beauty, even in what is broken.

Men who have experienced the pain of their mothers and fathers being taken out on them. Now living with the scars of not knowing how to give and receive love because of it.

Women not knowing how to uplift and embrace their men without the fear of being hurt for doing so.

Grown men, not knowing how to be good men because no one was ever a good man to them.

My mothers story does not stand alone.

Generational trauma comes in so many different forms.

I'm not here to point the finger or right anyone else's wrongs. I am here to say that no matter the pain that you have come from or experienced, you can rise above it.

It starts with understanding your strength and power and how to remove it from a place of pain to position it to efforts of loving, uplifting and bettering yourself.

No one on this earth can seek and find perfection. We can however act as leaders in acknowledging areas where growth is necessary and stepping up as change agents to evoke it.

Changing our communities starts with a commitment to changing ourselves. A commitment to healing what is broken and standing up for what is right. A commitment to putting an end to secrets and hidden shame and instead replacing it with dignity, growth and attempts at restoration.

It is your choice.

Break the chains of generational bondage, or re-live them in this embodiment or the next...

Save the Black Family, Save the Black Community.

We all have a part in this movement.

4.
ABUSED CHILDREN GROW UP TO BE CONFUSED ADULTS

Whether we care to admit it or not, the influence of a parent reaches well beyond childhood.

Every abandoned child's dream is to have a family.

I was too young to dream. Too young to know what was going on. As a baby, all that I remember was this ringing in my ears.

That, and an overwhelming feeling of sadness.

I was a child of the system as a toddler and was provided the foster care of a family that would raise me into my young adult years. Growing up, this family was the only family I ever knew.

Born Brittney Renee ****...

Adopted into a new identity - Nicole Brittney ****.

To this day, I've never seen pictures of myself as a baby or before the age of two.

When a child experiences abandonment as an infant, trauma reactions plague their reality for the rest of their lives.

I am no exception.

My upbringing, my past, my story, still hurt me to this day. As I actively work to mend the pain, it is important that I address the foundation of it.

I was not raised in a manner that I should be the woman you see today.

Yes, on the surface, I was blessed.

Blessed to have a family when my own neglected me. Blessed to grow up in the church. Blessed to be told, 'I love you' every night. Blessed that much of my upbringing was on the 'right side of town'.

Blessed to grow up in a big family where holiday's and family cook-outs were year 'round occasions.

Blessed to be a bright, shy, pretty, long-haired young girl.

Blessed on the surface but hiding demons behind closed doors.

As a child especially, I was always known as 'the polite girl'.

Quiet unless addressed. The empath. The light hearted and sensitive person who by any means aimed to keep the peace. I watched myself carry on this docile and sensitive approach well into adulthood, while people used and belittled me, right in front of my face.

I was the type of person who would allow disrespect after disrespect until my submissiveness turned to rage and helplessness. Only then would I take action.

This passive, keep the peace mindset was not only a product of nature, but nurture as well. I was molded into this way of thinking through fear and instigated insecurities at a very young age.

Deep down, I will never understand why people choose to care for children that they don't have the capacity to love. Is it ill intention, a lack of self control or a true absence of awareness?

> While I believe the family that raised me started out with good intentions, consistent action did not further that approach.
>
> I am a product of - if we walk into this store and you make a sound, I'll beat you.
>
> I am a product of - what goes on in this house stays in this house.
>
> I am a product of - because I said so!

> I am a product of - shut up, you sound stupid.
>
> I am a product of - do that again and I'll kill you.

I am a product of abuse.

For every dream that I had as a little girl, there were comments of how that would never be me. Taunting teases of why I wasn't good enough. Comments of why I should just sit down and shut up.

No, it wasn't always this way... but anyone who has dealt with abuse understands how it can overshadow much of the good. I am no different. I remember the good times. But more impactfully, I remember the bad.

I remember the nights in tears. The letters that I wrote, begging for change that were never addressed or even considered.

I remember the painful insults. I remember the pleasure derived from belittling me.

I remember being ostracized from children my own age and even my own siblings and family members. I remember being beaten for something as small as scratching my eczema or speaking out of line.

I remember watching my brothers and sisters being beaten, relentlessly.

Whipped, punched, stepped on and choked. Hearing cries and shrieks of pain behind closed doors.

I remember nights I didn't think we would live through.

I remember the fear that each and every one of us held deep down that hung like a cloud above our very existence.

I remember and still sense the internal shame and embarrassment.

I remember family members that turned a blind eye and made jokes about 'the warden'. Those who even listened to gossip and braggings about these beatings. Perhaps never realizing how intense and impactful these occurrences really were.

And then it's like one day the pages continued to turn, I grew up, my brothers and sisters grew up... the happenings were no longer mentioned and we were all just subliminally expected to forgive, forget and move on.

To act as if none of it ever happened at all...

Imagine how small a person would have to make themselves to do this.

These are the upbringings that so many of us don't acknowledge.

But the effects are apparent.

A slave mentality of parental control that breeds more abuse, more confusion, and little to no self respect.

Parents have so much of an influence on a child's experiences as an adult.

I am the eldest of my upbringing. A success story - on the surface.

Ironically, this is the same view that outsiders had of me as a little girl.

But just like that image of my childhood, it's all a facade.

The relationships that I've invested in as an adult have been mirror reflections of my experiences as a child.

I ran away from my hometown as a teenager. But, trauma knows no location or boundaries. Here it is my early thirties and I'm still mending what I experienced at the age of five.

All I can say is better late than never.

And it's never too late.

Sharing and addressing the hurt that you've experienced at the hands of another will always come with exposure. It will always come with one side of the coin expressing their memories at the expense of the other. But, whether it be in a journal, a counseling session, a one-on-one discussion, or some other platform that you see fit, *you deserve to free yourself.*

It is not my intention to hurt or belittle anyone. I know deep down that we all have our own pain and sometimes it is easy to take that pain out on the people closest to us.

As the saying goes, 'hurt people, hurt people'...

However, addressing our hurt is an important aspect of healing.

So many of us educate away the pain, travel away the pain, party away the pain, sex away the pain, drink or drug away the pain, work away the pain, run away the pain...

But at the core of our being, the pain becomes our insecurities, our limitations and our rage.

When we don't address what's hurt us, we become an embodiment of it in one way or another.

I want to see more of us be freed.

I want to see more of us seek the healing we so desperately need and deserve.

To begin, I had to start with myself.

I learned to love this family with the love I had hoped to experience myself.

In doing so, a path to healing for us all was laid.

Love is a healer.

I want even those who have harmed to be healed.

Maybe then there will be less victims.

Maybe then there will be less tears shed.

Maybe then there will be far less children that grow up to be adults that abuse others or are abused themselves.

Maybe then we will all begin to know and understand our worth.

5.

EMOTIONAL WARFARE

Where does emotional warfare end and healing begin?

Consider the following three stories...

1. Dominique was exhausted. She's counted on her mother time and time again for support but she was never there when she needed her. Dominique was now stuck at the doctor's office with her three children, the youngest suffering from an ear infection and hot to the touch with a fever. As Dominique tried to console her sick and crying baby girl, she scrambled to keep her two sons close and quiet. They were tired from being dragged from place to place all day and ran, played

and bickered until Dominique thought she might lose it! Her mother had promised her the night before that she'd watch the boys so Dominique could take her youngest to the doctor in peace. Yet, when she called that morning, no answer.

Her mother wasn't there for her when she was a child. Her grandmother raised her while her mother did who knows what. Even when her mother was present in her upbringing, Dominique only saw her drunk, cussing out some man….or worse. The least her mother could do is be there for her grandchildren.

After her grandmother's death Dominique's mother sobered up and with the help of a family counselor the mother and daughter worked to mend their relationship. Dominique had hoped for some support from her mother as she was a newly single mother herself and just trying to figure things out. Instead, all Dominique ever seemed to get from her mother was apologies and broken promises.

She looked to her purse where she felt her phone vibrating. She picked up the phone to her mothers sobbing apologies about oversleeping and car trouble. Her mother wanted to stop by and get the boys now. She also asked for gas money and help with groceries… Are you serious?! Dominique rolled her eyes. She was the one suffering, she was the one who needed a mother! Yet all she ever got was disappointment.

Yes, her mother tried, but honestly…. It was never enough to truly make a difference.

2. After months of counseling and separation, Jillian and her husband John decided to move back in together to repair their marriage. The couple had two beautiful children together and wanted nothing more than to raise them in a healthy and loving environment. Jillian battled with post traumatic stress disorder and low self esteem that stemmed from her abusive childhood. John knew that she didn't mean to be hurtful but when Jillian experienced a trigger she tended to go into these deep and dark states of depression and rage that sent their whole household into a state of chaos.

Ongoing counseling revealed that Jillian was not only suffering from PTSD but bi-polar disorder as well. More recently, she began to fantasize that John had been cheating on her. When he was away at work she became increasingly obsessed with this idea and that he was not only cheating on her but also planning to leave her for another woman. This insecurity sent her into fits of rage, depression and attempts at taking her own life.

These episodes had serious effects on the family.

Jillian's last outburst led to her husband enrolling her in a mental health facility in hopes that she could receive the professional help that she needed to begin healing from her broken past.

After seven months of counseling, Jillian's doctors signed for her release and guaranteed that with her new medication and ongoing counseling, she would continue to see improvement.

The couple moved back in together and for a while, things were perfect. But after a very long and stressful workday, John came home to a hysterical Jillian, a state that he had not witnessed her in for almost a year at this point.

John was scared.

'*Will she ever really change*', he thought.

He considered whether or not this should be his final sign to leave his wife for good.

3. Ashley was tired of her sister's shit. This chick doesn't care about anyone but herself!!! Ashley was convinced!

   The Jackson family had planned a surprise birthday party for their dear great aunt and Brittany, Ashley's sister, was in charge of decorations and the cake.

   The party was starting at 5PM and it was already 4:07 that afternoon.

   '*We might as well just cancel*', Ashely thought.

   There was no way they could decorate the banquet hall for the event in an hour. Just as Ashley pulled out her phone to start making calls to cancel, in strolled Brittany, free as a bird and with no decorations or cake in sight.

"*Brittany, where is the cake? Where are the decorations?*" Ashley asked.

"*Chill sis, they're in the car...*" Brittany rolled her eyes and plopped down in an empty chair.

"Brittany, can we get a move on this? We've still got to decorate and family will start arriving any minute!"

"*Here you go! Uptight Ashley, everything by the deadline. So damn boring and predictable. Here!*" Brittany handed over the keys to Ashley, got up and stood in front of the banquet hall's body length mirror and began primping her curls.

Ashley thought to herself, '*this is the last straw*'. Brittany was always throwing jabs at Ashley and always acting like she was better than everyone else.

Brittany was the favorite of the family. Growing up Ashley was treated like the stepchild while Brittany pounced around like the queen. Their mother had set them against each other from the start and Ashley knew it wasn't Brittany's fault... but she seemed to have picked up every toxic trait their mother had.

Diva, selfish, uncaring, unhelpful and stuck up.

Mind you neither of the women had it good growing up. There were family secrets that they both experienced that had never been addressed... But still. Enough was enough. Ashley had turned out to be a good person. Brittany had to decide to do the same for herself, as far as Ashley was concerned.

She was convinced her sister would never change....

Many of us, at some point or another in our lifetime, have suffered from or witnessed an unhealthy relationship.

Perhaps, yours was similar to one of the three stories shared here.

Maybe it was better, maybe it was worse.

Either way, we've all been in a place where we've had to decide whether or not to leave or repair a challenging relationship.

How do you choose whether you should forgive or walk away?

How do you aim to find peace in unpeaceful circumstances?

Emotional warfare is at the heart of so many of our stories and experiences. From childhood on into adulthood, many of us have seen trauma for the majority of our lives. Even those with peaceful upbringings have likely crossed paths with an unhealthy friend, partner or even associate.

Trying to decipher a good and healthy relationship from one that is not can become more and more confusing with each and every traumatic experience that we face.

If you had the following three scenarios occur within your life and you could only save one of the three relationships, which would you choose, and why?

Take some time to think deeply about this.

Are some unhealthy relationships worth saving? Are they all? Should we remove from our lives every one who disappoints us? Or, should we have a heart of understanding and help them to change?

These are questions that most of us have considered at one time or another in our lives...

Now - look deep within yourself.

Have you ever disappointed a loved one? Have you ever hurt someone close to you out of frustration or a need to release your own painful energy? If some of our loved ones looked back on our treatment of them, would they consider leaving us and investing in a more healthy relationship *themselves*?

These are necessary reflections and the beginning stages to having a heart to heart with yourself about your life and the state of your relationships.

Many of us are carrying pain that we need to let go of and many of us are dragging by the knees at relationships that have chained our ankles to the ground.

It is important that we begin to ask ourselves these questions and define the necessary boundaries that help to make room for our own personal growth.

What relationships need to be evaluated within your life?

Where does emotional warfare end and healing begin?

It starts with an acknowledgement of the state of our relationships. Identifying challenging relationships and uncovering opportunities to heal or distance ourselves where necessary.

We must also consider and be honest with ourselves about the levels of dysfunction we might have added to our own personal relationships now and in the past.

Love heals and love cancels out a multitude of sins, sure!

But the truth of the matter is that we cannot fully love and embrace one another if we are holding onto internal pain and relationships that continue to drain us.

We have to consider a new way of addressing these circumstances.

Many of the unhealthy relationships we have in our lives stem from an unhealthy mental state, a lack of awareness around emotional intelligence and the pain individuals have experienced and not healed from. I don't believe that people are born into this world in a state of rage or hate but that they instead develop these tendencies from an inability to cope from unfortunate life experiences.

But these circumstances do not alleviate personal responsibility.

Whatever the reason may be, many of us don't know how to turn the hurt and frustration that we feel inside into something productive and empowering. Therefore, we release that energy in hurting, competing with and belittling the people around us and in doing so, we damage our communities as a whole.

ACCOUNTABILITY PART I

I encourage you to take a deliberate but very compassionate approach to your healing and the healing of your personal relationships and bonds.

Look back at your own life and relationships.

Uncover the motives behind your deepest relationships. Do you pursue love and harmony or are you often attracted to chaos and dysfunction? Is it a mix of both or do you lean closer to one end of the spectrum or the other?

Be honest with yourself about your ability to love and engage in healthy relationships.

If you consider that there are areas of opportunity and healing within your own life, pursue them. You can change and you can heal but it will be easier with the right resources, education and support. Don't be afraid to invest in your own healing.

You must be the change you wish to see before expecting to see that change in anyone else.

ACCOUNTABILITY PART II

Next, consider relationships within your life that are in need of repair.

Is there hope for change, or are you attached to relationships that no longer serve you?

Again, be honest with yourself. Making excuses or ignoring red flags will come at your own expense.

It is time for us to start addressing our unhealthy bonds with a more educated and deliberate approach to healing.

It's okay to say, *this person hurt me so deeply, I am not sure if I can ever have a healthy relationship with them to follow.*

It's also okay to say, *I know this person has treated me wrong, but I believe there are resources that can help us to better communicate with each other about the past and develop a more healthy relationship in the future.*

For each relationship that you choose to repair, make sure you use the same approach that you would use to heal yourself, individually. Develop healthy boundaries. Be mindful to not allow the relationship to stunt your own individual growth and healing during the process of repair. Utilize resources and have support systems in place that you can go to for counsel.

For those relationships that you must let go of, do so humbly.

This is someone you once loved and may still love who might be suffering from their own life experiences. You can wish them all the best while continuing to pursue a healthier, more whole and more healed you.

Hold your head up high and congratulate yourself on taking healthy steps towards your own healing and deliverance. We are the generation of change.

There are so many resources available to us to help us to better understand and mend unhealthy habits, relationships, and states of mind.

Once you begin the path to healing, you empower not only yourself but everyone around you.

My path to healing offered me the ability to plant seeds in areas I once only dreamed of. In doing so, good favor has come to my life and whether I walk alone or with a tribe of survivors, I am at peace with myself.

Heal yourself.

Let go of relationships that no longer serve you.

Repair and love on those that make sense.

This is the start to your new beginning.

Laying the foundation for a healthier family starts with you.

6.

A TIME TO HEAL

Allowing Past Pain to Uplift (My Own Self Reflection)

This is a very interesting week for me…

A week where I am fortunate enough to look back on what I've gone through with humility and ebbs and flows of both sadness and joy.

It's my birthweek.

I can thank none other than the God above for seeing me this far.

With every obstacle that I have received, I have aimed to position it as a source of strength rather than to consider it a burden.

This has become all that I, like so many others, have learned to do...

This will be my first holiday season as a newly single woman.

Single and delivered.

While the current pandemic won't allow for a trip home, I am thankful for the opportunity to reflect and continue to heal.

Several years ago, I experienced a birthday that rocked my world. What should have been a celebratory milestone for me was instead made a miserable memory. One that I still need to let go of and offer forgiveness in my heart for today. While I am no longer angry at the occurrence, it still hurts the depths of my heart that I had to experience it.

A small weekend brunch celebration transformed into a quiet storm.

As my partner and I said our goodbyes to a small group of family and friends, belittlement and taunting began in just a matter of moments. Echos of insults still ring in my ears...

> *Of how the people we celebrated with weren't really there for me, didn't love me, how he could easily have his pick of any number of my girlfriends. Of how I wasn't as pretty as I thought I was.... The list went on.*

I'm a happy woman by nature, a celebrator. I have a strength within me that I couldn't tell you where it was derived from. I knew my partner, I knew his ways, and though the words cut deep, they were not a new occurrence and I was determined to continue to celebrate myself internally, whether he cared to do so with me or not.

We made it home where he retreated to the bedroom to rest. I sat and reflected in the living room alone. It was about midday and the Sunday before my birthday. I began to grow sad.

Despite being home with my significant other, I felt lonely. I needed affection and began to yearn for it badly.

I stepped into the bedroom like a child, mild mannered and meek in tone, asking my partner what was wrong. I was determined to approach this with understanding. I asked him if there was anything that I could do to help him feel better.

He remained silent, fiddling with his phone. I was ignored.

I crawled onto the bed and tried to cuddle. This display of affection was not reciprocated so I got onto my knees and began to beg, '*could we please do something else with our afternoon. Could we please take some time to enjoy each other and celebrate one on one, together*'….

I didn't see it coming.

I didn't expect or anticipate but my partner's next move was a back hand strike to my face that sent me flying off of our canopy bed and to the floor.

I will remember this moment for the rest of my life.

The moment I truly realized the state of my relationship.

I sat on the floor in silence.

I remember this attack as far different than any other.

I did not cry for help, I did not lash back out, I did not sob or say a word.

I sat, stars ringing in my vision and my ears. I remained on the floor in a daze.

I recall it being around sunset by this time as the room began to grow dark. He continued to lay in the bed. After about five minutes, I left the room, retreated back into the living room, sat still, barely even thinking. Some hour or so later, I took myself on a drive....

Physically, my marriage did not end until years later, but spiritually, it ended that day.

My birthday came and went a day or so later. I spent it in silence. Shut off from the world. One side of my face colored a dark purple and black where the initial welt had turned to a bruise.

A piece of me died that day. A piece of me that I may never truly recover from.

I realized that if I could not be celebrated on something as special as a milestone, I would never be celebrated for the woman that I was, in that relationship.

This marked the climax of my final life season with abuse. This was where I decided deep down inside of me, enough was enough. I would not stand to be belittled at the hands of one more person, in this life or the next.

So many of life's experiences are just not fair.

....To loving someone who doesn't love you the same. To losing someone you love to death, illness or incarceration. To being disappointed that something you deserved was given to another. To not having the strength to believe in yourself in a way that actually brings about results....

We all have our stories. We all have our defeats.

This story is not just a story of abuse. It is the story of a moment in weakness.

It is the cry that lives deep within us all. The cry urging us to give up, urging us to just stop trying, to move on, to grow hardened and cold. Anything we can do or become to replace the pain.

How easy it is to fall into a state of darkness.

How much effort it takes to stand up and run from it.

I am thankful that I found the strength to stand up and to run.

I am thankful that I used my experiences to teach me better rather than to cement my feet to my own living grave.

Death is not just a physical state of being. I see so many that have died inside while still walking this earth in the flesh. Sometimes, even with a smile...

Yes, this memory hurts. Perhaps it always will. But this memory also empowers my journey, my purpose and my being.

I am more than anything this world can throw at me.

And you my dear are too.

May the light within you continue to shine out even the darkest of memories and experiences.

Never forget your worth.

Always muster up even a step in the direction towards strength and upliftment.

One day you will look back and realize you climbed a whole mountain, if even on the foundation of your very own tears.

Part II

UNDERSTANDING OUR CURRENT STRUGGLES

What we make of our current circumstances sets in motion what we receive in the future.

It is not enough to just heal from the past.

If we are not able to come to terms with ourselves and how we should navigate the present, our futures will be at risk.

Life will never be all rainbows and flowers, no matter how good of a person we are and no matter how hard we try. There will always be a new challenge, a new limitation and a new hardship, right around the corner.

Choosing to approach these situations with rage, insecurity and immaturity will only further the possibility of pain.

Everything in this life is meant to teach us.

We can be the stubborn student who chooses not to learn or thinks they are above it all, or we can humble ourselves and begin to look at each obstacle and experience from a third person perspective and take action according to reason instead of solely being fueled by emotion.

If we are not able to master our approach to life, we will be led by it and not the masters of it.

SELF REFLECTION:

As you read the following stories - consider your current life's approach.

- Do you truly love yourself, just as you are?
- Do you have a plan in place for your continued healing?
- How do you currently deal with challenges and triggers?
- Are you struggling with insecurities that may be limiting your ability to grow?
- Are you looking at your own life through the lens of others?
- Are you using certain actions or activities to draw your attention away from pain?
- Is there a healthier process that you can implement to help you deal with life's obstacles?
- Are you presenting the 'you' that you want this world to experience?

7.

OVERCOMING OBSTACLES

Life disappointments come a dime a dozen.

Some we might expect. Others seem to come out of the blue.

From vacation plans that change or are cancelled at the last minute; To receiving bad news from a friend; To loved ones lying and breaking your trust; To failing a test you knew you studied hard for; To receiving that unexpected call that someone you love has passed away...

Disappointments come in a wide variety of forms and often at the most unprecedented times.

Dealing with difficulty when you are already on a downward trajectory can feel overwhelming.

There were times in my life where I felt so buried in my circumstances, that giving up seemed like the most logical thing to do.

It's easy to get lost in thoughts of doubt...

> *Maybe if I didn't care so much, the disappointments wouldn't feel as burdensome.*
>
> *Maybe I'm not who I think I am.*
>
> *Maybe I'm not meant for the success I'm working towards.*

If I had chosen to feed a mindset of doubt, I wouldn't be writing to you today.

Giving up is the easiest thing to do.

While life does come with shouldering the brunt of some hardship - change, disappointments and challenges offer opportunities to shape and mold us into something greater.

Life takes courage.

It takes courage at the times we might feel our weakest.

It takes courage when everything around us is tumbling down to stand up and make calculated decisions to help catch a few of the bricks being tossed our way, and use them to build, instead of letting them crush us to smithereens.

What we do in these defining moments is what propels us forward, or what keeps us stagnant and comfortable.

Stepping outside of your comfort zone, into the unknown, forces you to make decisions that you usually would not, which in turn allows your mind to expand to new territories.

Standing courageous against adversity is what transforms your identity from the familiar to an exploration of the unknown. The unknown, that even when met with failure or defeat, will still lead you to growth and a deeper understanding of yourself and the world around you.

Truth is not what you are told, what you read, or what you study.

Truth is what you are willing to experience and learn for yourself.

Truth varies by person. Truth is what is real to *you.*

So in all reality, life's challenges are our hidden blessings.

They are an opportunity to rise to the occasion and meet difficulty with a new approach.

> *Challenges offer an opportunity to learn more about yourself and the world around you.*

Obstacles are an opportunity to defy the odds and rise as a conqueror.

Hardships are the stepping stones to success.

Disappointments are the cornerstones to improved character.

Opposition offers an opportunity to level up to a you you've never experienced before.

Everything in life is a product of our approach and mindset.

Your mind is a sword and your experiences act as a sharpener.

Ignoring an opportunity to sharpen your tool will lead to a dull and useless weapon in the long run.

Meeting each of life's obstacles with courage and hope, no matter the outcome, offers an opportunity to sharpen the wits of your mind.

You are only as strong as you allow yourself to be.

May the best soldiers WIN.

8.

TRIGGERED

My heart dropped as I watched a story that seemed all too familiar to me.

It wasn't my story....

But in that moment - my body, my heart and my mind couldn't tell the difference.

Shots ringing through my ears as if I were there.

I stood, feet frozen to the ground as I watched this unfamiliar man being shot in the back by the police in his own backyard.

Killed, and aired without warning, in a manner to me that seemed more like entertainment than news.

I held my breath so long I thought I'd pass out.

My mind went blank, my vision blurred, by body numb.

It hurt so bad, you couldn't tell me that wasn't my own brother on that television screen.

I haven't turned on the TV to watch the news or even a documentary *ever* since...

In later years, as I grew to recover and reshape my life, I learned that this moment was the epitome of a trigger.

In 2008, I lost my big brother to gun violence.

It wasn't at the hands of the police, but his own brother. A young and lost soul who grew up in the same community, moved by ignorance, boredom and possibly his own self hatred, released on another soul.

Death, murder and suicide were a normal part of life in my hometown.

As I watched this stranger, shot multiple times in what should have been the security of his own home, all that I could think, feel and smell was my own brother.

The gun that ended his life.

His cry for help.

His tears, and the thoughts that must have wandered his mind as he realized he was taking the last breaths of his very young and sweet life...

Holding my breath, turned to shortness of breath, turned to panic and an overwhelming state of stress that I couldn't escape.

Feelings of anxiety encompassed my being in a very familiar way.

Suddenly, this was more than just a stranger on the local news.

This, to my mind and body, was the difference between life and death.

It was as if my mind had left reality and my body followed suit.

The hairs on my arms danced to life and my heartbeat raced to a new tune.

I remember feeling as if I myself might pass out or even die at that very moment.

I've had many similar instances as this within my life.

Not only at the memory of the loss of my dear brother, but at other, impactful and traumatizing experiences that have passed physically but left deep scars on my psychological state of being.

True realizations that the experiences that shaped my life, would always be a part of my life, no matter how far removed in location, time or healing that I was.

For a greater part of my adulthood I struggled with this.

Struggled with feelings of panic, insecurity and doubt.

Mentally reliving circumstances that were no longer a part of my current state of being.

I struggled with anxiety that I thought would go away when moving to a new location or starting a new job. But instead the anxiety haunted me in unexpected spurts of heart palpitations, difficulty breathing, overwhelming feelings of guilt, shame, confusion and rage.

There were chapters in my life where I seemed to live in a state of panic. Sometimes, taking on the smallest activities and experiences left me with heavy feelings of doubt and resentment. Insecurity within myself and a lack of trust in those around me.

Feelings that I thought would go away with time, success and new love but instead haunted every walk of my life that I allowed until I was strong enough to address them.

At a time, this part of recovery scared the hell out of me.

The realization that I may never truly shake triggering feelings all together was something that I had to come to terms with. To this day, I still have days where it's difficult to eat, days where it's difficult to accept myself. Days where I feel I must be doing something wrong, even if little to nothing is really going on in my life.

This is a product of trauma and my previous experiences.

I used to want to drown my pain with new activities, people and a lack of acknowledgement of what I was feeling inside.

But as I grew to heal, I realized that this approach would never truly fix the internal stress that I was experiencing. Instead, ignoring and not dealing with my pain only prolonged the effects of my past circumstances.

If I was going to truly find healing, I had to stop pacifying the pain and find an approach to understand and deal with it instead.

Many survivors of trauma have experienced this same level of distress and discomfort.

Trauma changes the structure of the survivors brain and thought process. Acknowledging these new mental states is the first step to learning how to cope and transition to a healthier state of being.

I wish that I could tell you it's easy.

I wish that I could tell you just leaving that traumatic relationship or growing from that hurtful experience will take away all your pain.

But, the truth of the matter is that the time and growth between you and your state of trauma only serve as a natural first step to overcoming. There will be many other steps that you will need to take to deliberately lead you to a more healthy and recovered you.

It's a process and the only thing that will truly move the needle on the process, is time, patience and an understanding of yourself and how your experiences have shaped and left a mark on you.

Some days it will feel like you can't breath. Other days, you will celebrate making the best decision of your life and overcoming some new obstacle that you were not able to in prior times.

You have to hold your head high and your back straight and accept every moment of your recovery - the joy, the confusion and the pain. With that courage, you will begin to learn the deeper you and uncover aspects of yourself that may still be vulnerable to a future encounter with trauma.

Healing isn't just walking away and wiping your hands clean of the past.

Healing is standing toe to toe with your deepest and darkest self and being honest with yourself about the mark that trauma left on your life.

You must accept and acknowledge the past for exactly the devil it was to you.

It may be difficult, but you *must* identify your triggers.

Understanding your triggers is a part of under-standing the new you.

9.

FINDING INNER PEACE

My college years marked a very odd time in my life.

Odd is the only logical word that I can draw upon to describe the strange and seemingly surreal experiences that occurred during this time and the sense of pure emptiness that I was left with.

In a matter of just a couple of years I lost my grandmother, my father and my brother.

Years that were supposed to be marked with education, expanding opportunities and new friendships included a storm of multiple other changes within the structure of my life and familial line that I did not truly know how to process.

I remember the feelings that each loss brought with it. I was not a highly emotionally expressive young person and while I felt sadness within my heart, it was not something I knew how to express outwardly to others.

I felt very misunderstood. I carried the weight of each experience internally and learned to just move forward with each day and accept the harder days in silent tears and the happier moments in the company of my peers at school.

My fathers passing brought a strange sense of emptiness and confusion to this time and truly left me in a state of solitude, unable to express not even a moment of how the inner me felt to anyone in my outside world.

I met my father around the age of fifteen.

Growing up adopted, I remember wandering through my neighborhood, the grocery store and other local places looking strangers in the eyes and wondering if they might be my mother or father.

I always yearned to have an understanding of who I was and why I was the way that I was.

I always felt....different.

I knew that one day meeting my mother and father would give me a glimpse into all of the gaps in my story that I grew tired of filling with my imagination alone.

Finally, the day to meet my father came.

This opportunity was special to me. I felt drawn to this man that I didn't even know but who looked just like me and seemed so familiar. In my heart of hearts, I yearned to be close to him, to build a relationship with him and to understand everything about him and his walk.

Our interactions during that time however, were short lived. As soon as I met him it seemed like even less time passed where we were saying goodbye. Being his only daughter, it felt to me that he aimed to connect with my brothers, but was more hesitant and unaware of how to connect with his only little girl, me.

While we maintained a relationship through writing letters and emails, the thought was always that we would connect on a deeper level at some other, more purposeful time in the future.

When I received the very unanticipated news of his death, I felt a sadness within me that struck suddenly and took all of the light out of my world.

An isolated summer storm on a seemingly perfect day...

I retreated within myself and felt every moment of that pain in the confines of my mind.

I was not able to be a part of my fathers funeral because he was many hours away and I did not have transportation or any relationships with that side of the family.

I could not express myself to my brothers because they had more dissociated feelings with my fathers passing and were not emotionally available.

The family that raised me had no particular opinion or emotional connection to the occurrence as he might as well have been a stranger to them.

Despite my not intimately knowing my father, a part of me felt that I had lost my whole world.

Prior to his death, I just knew there would always be a time in the future where I'd be able to make memories and learn about this man that I knew deep down was my kindred spirit.

His death marked not only the inability to grow a bond with him physically but also a mental inability to learn the depths of myself and why I was the way that I was from his eyes.

It felt so very unfair.

I recall feeling for a long stunt in time that this might as well have been the end of my very existence. I would never learn the depths of my soul and I would never be able to make up for the lost childhood that I should have had with my father.

This death felt like the end of a chapter in my book of life. A chapter that I found a very hard time recovering and moving forward from. A climax filled with defeat.

I have never, to this day, expressed these thoughts.

I have never acknowledged the state of rage and confusion that I feel at life and the happenings of the universe for allowing my story to unfold in this way.

Until this day.

I always thought that good reigned true.

That life would be as good to you as you were to it.

Especially in my younger years.

I thought that my decision to take the road less traveled and to pursue higher education, instead of the statistical approach to life in my community, would alleviate me from hardship and illuminate my path from the darkness I had experienced in my past.

I did not anticipate or know how to process and bring peace to myself during this season of hardship.

I did not know that it was my responsibility to do so.

These ideas made accepting the death that occured in this season of my life almost unbearable.

Oftentimes, we consider peace as something someone else should give us.

Something we deserve for some trait or some experience that we surpassed.

We assume that peace is granted based on the goodness of our heart and that outside factors should bend and fold and offer us praises of peace and blessings based on what we know of ourselves.

But this is not the way that life works...

Planting seeds of goodness does ensure their return in one way or another, but it is not a get out of jail free card from hardships and the occurrences of trials and tribulations.

Peace is not something that life just hands you in a shiny and impressive gift box wrapped with a bow.

Peace is something you create for yourself.

Peace is a manifestation of you.

Peace is something you must learn to draw upon in even the most trivial of times.

Life will go on and sometimes you may find yourself submerged in chaos that you did nothing to create...

Still, if peace is within you, it will show itself true in the deepest and darkest of circumstances.

You must learn how to find your inner peace and manifest it each and every day.

Inner peace is what will light even the darkest days.

Peace is a state of mind.

Peace is a state of being.

Once you tap into your God-given place of peace, it becomes a comfort and place of refuge that can never be taken away from you.

10.

NON-COMPETE AGREEMENT

...Without even thinking, I moved forward again.

Slam. Woosh!!!!

My head shot back with a quickness.

My body jerked with it and the next thing I knew I shot three feet back.

Stunned and dazed, I moved forward again.

Pow. Boom.

Damnit.

Fuck.

As courageous as my heart was, I just couldn't catch a break.

Hit with a shot to the body that sent me tumbling down.

Ding, ding, ding.

Round over.

Thank God!…..

As I caught my breath my coach lined me up for another -

"Get your head in the game! Three more rounds to go!"

My first day sparring. As ready as I thought I was, that night proved otherwise. I was lined up with a room full of young Muay Thai fighters who seemed all too eager to spar and have fun with the new kid in the room.

"Your offense is good but your defense sucks."

"Those boys were having fun with me! They knew I was new to this!"

"So what! You're wearing your heart all over your face. Walking right into their punches. Of course they're going to shoot. You've got heart, but you've got to level up and think in this game if you're going to ever win."

I'll never forget that moment.

One of the most fun and humiliating nights of my career pursuing boxing.

While I've always considered myself athletically inclined and more often than not the sharpest person in most of my fitness endeavors; in boxing, this was just not the case.

There were others who had trained and studied longer and harder, and to even compete, I'd have to put in the work and invest my time and effort.

I was humbled.

What I thought would come natural and quick to me would instead take months if not possibly years to master.

Life....

Fitness and specifically, boxing - shaped a new chapter of my life that was necessary and somewhat painful (yes, both mentally and physically).

It changed me.

Instead of being so outwardly focused and impulsive, I began to grow a more internally peaceful and patience outlook on my life.

I've always had a somewhat obsessive personality.

This proved to be a downfall in approaching this sport.

I wanted my progress to come quickly.

I had no patience or tolerance for losing or looking bad.

While this was helpful in fueling my work ethic, it was an unrealistic expectation and an attitude that blocked many opportunities for me to learn from defeat.

You have to be willing to lose, sometimes...

There is no environment in life where you will be the best one in the room, every time.

There will always be someone stronger, smarter, more clever, more good looking, more insightful, *more something*, than you.

Get comfortable with that and don't run from it.

Oftentimes, I see others not willing to share their expertise, not willing to teach others, not willing to share their secrets, because of a fear that someone else will beat them in their own game.

This is the very mindset that's limited us as a people and discouraged collective growth.

Not only do we as individuals want to be the best, we don't even want to be in the room with someone that could possibly threaten our success.

We act as if success is of a limited quantity and only available to a select few.

We do not act with a mindset of abundance.

So we limit the next man's growth while also limiting ours...

You cannot grow in a place of comfortability.

You cannot grow without placing yourself in challenging environments that you approach with openness.

You cannot grow if you are not willing to have strong and intelligent people around who are capable of competing.

In limiting ourselves to such, *we* remain the same.

I never knew how limited my mindset truly was until I stepped into this unknown world, invested in mentors and trainers who knew much more than me, and became willing to fall on my face and lose - until I got better.

Losing propels further success, *if we let it.*

Surrounding ourselves with weakness just to be the only one in the room who shines, should be a thing of the past….

We must be willing to surround ourselves with greatness so that we ALL might grow.

11.

CONFIDENCE IS KEY

The journey to restoring your confidence is a beautiful and necessary part of recovering from trauma.

After realizing the toxic trends in my relationships and making a deliberate decision to invest in healthier love, this aspect of my journey was the most critical in enabling me to present myself as a whole and healed woman to myself and future relationships.

You have to be alright with you before you can expect to flourish and be confident and comfortable in the arms of another. You have to be alright with you to walk upright and deal with all the challenges and circumstances that life is going to throw at you.

Deep down, I knew this to be true and I wanted to invest in a path to a more comfortable and confident, me.

When you have suffered at the hands of trauma or abuse, you have been limited as a human being in one way or another.

For years of my engagements with abuse, I lived in a box.

I limited my self-expression to please others.

I felt that if I was too confident, too much of myself, I might intimidate those around me and not be an appealing woman to be around. I aimed to blend in instead of stand out. This is what many partners and friends within my life's walk had expressed to me as *more desirable.*

So, as much as possible, I aimed to limit and soften my presence, rather than to shine as the true and divine woman that I was.

This is something I see being taught to children within our communities quite often. Especially in some given religious environments. This idea that humility and lessening our 'louder' attributes is more pleasing to God and others than to live too carefree, bold and free...

So I, like many, from childhood on into my romantic and professional life, limited myself.

Limited myself professionally. Limited myself in the presence of girlfriends and sometimes even admirers. Limited myself for the security of others. Limited myself so that no one in the room would feel threatened.

Limited myself to 'be fair'.

This can be dangerous.

It's dangerous because every individual has an inner being that must be expressed.

It's not just your personality but your identity. It's what sets you apart and how you show yourself value in the flesh.

Limiting your being, has psychological effects that can be detrimental to our mindsets and acceptance of self.

We as individuals are unique beyond reason.

You cannot truly love and master yourself if you limit what makes you, you.

You must learn to express yourself, freely.

Looking back I realized, I martyred myself.

The seeds that were planted in my mind as a child, fueled my approach to love which then led to a stronger foundation for similar approaches to other aspects of my life as well.

I found myself limiting my self expression romantically, in friendships, social settings and even professionally.

With each instance of sacrificing myself for the benefit of others, there was less and less and less of *me*.

There was a point in my life where I found myself very lost and empty.

I felt worthless.

None of the self-sacrificing that I did ever served me as an individual. It didn't truly limit conflict in my life and while it might have eased the tension of others, it didn't allow me to display my strengths or express my most unique self.

It only served to limit me and the light I had to offer this world.

I was bland, boring and looked to be just like everyone else.

Lost...

I remember feeling like a puppet. Confused about my very existence.

It was not enough to just turn from abusive relationships, I had to restore the me that was lost in the midst of them all as well.

I had to relearn self expression and explore the depths of myself.

Building my confidence and investing in my own self worth laid the foundation for me to celebrate myself whether alone or with a tribe of friends and family.

I learned to live for myself and not for the comforts and adoration of others.

I found myself better equipped to invest in more fruitful relationships as a result.

Build your confidence. Celebrate yourself and your accomplishments. Stand tall, even when faced with defeat.

Don't be afraid to invest in you.

BATTLEGROUND

An Ode to Strength in the Midst of Chaos

What about those battles -
Where you can't claim victory OR defeat?

Just even skies in the distance -
bleak, but promising if you can just look past:

The right now
the why's and the how's.

All those unanswered questions...

Too busy dwelling on the have nots -
those emotional stops, drops, holds.... disgust...

In all the things you don't have the power to control.

But at the same time feeling on top in the sense -
That no one can quite knock you off the pedestal you've built

While dropping down,
down,
DOWN.

Up again.

Then down -

around -

sometimes pounded into the ground!

But then back up.

Because it becomes all you know how to do.

Survive or be Eaten.

...but the predator is never devoured by its prey...

Weakend and distraught - life will have you

but don't let it be about who wins or who will lose!

Who stands strong?

Who walks those valleys and even in defeat carries on!!

Even in victory
—can consider the whispers of them ALL.
Kings and Queens, Gods and Goddesses
have fallen victim to worldly things.

But even the *peasant* who shows strength -

> ...when the world around them is nothing more than ruins and sad remains…

Should be alright and feel *damn good*
with their PEACE

right. in. between.

Part III

WALKING IN THE GLORY THAT IS YOU

Staring our past in the eyes took strength.

Being realistic about our current state of affairs took courage.

Moving forward in what is meant for you will take grace.

You have always, and will always, have everything you need to survive and to thrive, within the realms of your very being.

You are perfect just as you are. The only thing that is up for consideration is your ability to acknowledge your worth and use your gifts for good, *consistently.*

You must make what you have learned an improved way of life.

Perhaps the only thing that's ever needed to change, was your mental state of being.

Great care and consideration manifested life into your soul and body. You must show great care and consideration in protecting, preserving and growing the beautiful being that is you.

There is only one you.

Walking in a love for yourself is the greatest seed that you can plant.

Your peace, your talents, your wisdom and intelligence, transcend to everyone around you.

When people see a smiling and joyful you, it is a reflection of what they can strive to be as well.

Be magical. Be strong. Be deliberate.

Walk in grace and glory. There is no one like you.

Walking in glory changes not only you, but everyone and everything that you touch in this world as a result...

SELF REFLECTION:

As you read the following stories - be realistic about yourself and envision the future you.

Consider:

- Do you truly love yourself, just as you are?
- How are you showing yourself love?
- Are you changing your values/actions based on your environment or standing strong in your truth, no matter the circumstances?
- If there are changes that you would like to see in your life, have you put a plan in place to reach them?
- How do you plan to sustain yourself long term?
- How will you continue to evaluate your growth?

12.

REDEFINING WHAT YOU WILL ACCEPT

Even through the virtual screen I could see my face turning a shade of red that I began trying hard to calm down.

I could feel myself getting hot with frustration and everything inside of me trying to keep from shaking.

Here we go...

Another instance of my being belittled, publicly, in the workplace, and now, in front of a client.

I had a discussion with my leadership team weeks in advance, around my need for autonomy and to not be interrupted, unknowingly, during presentations and work meetings.

Yet, in the midst of a deal breaking presentation with my client, that was going amazing, might I add - my boss interjected with a huge win that I was saving for a special place within the discussion.

Internally, I was livid.

I caught myself in the present moment and deflected from my visible state of irritation to get back on topic and keep the presentation rolling. The worst thing that I could do was let anyone involved see me sweat.

While this instance derailed the meeting a bit, I had learned through experience, to save some of my secrets from even my boss so that I could still deliver and provide my expertise. This was not a new instance but something that I would have to learn to conquer during my time in leadership on this particular team.

Fast forward to my current state of professional affairs:

I have grown my career in corporate America for many years and while I continue to have a love and passion for what I do professionally, it's come with its ups and downs, specifically around my ability to draw boundaries and encourage a respectful seat at the table.

As a black woman in this environment, it doesn't always come easy.

I would describe myself as a collaborator and team player who aims to get the job done and done well, at all costs. My dedication to understanding and delivering on my responsibilities has helped to propel me forward and elevate my career. More often than not, I show myself as a leader and have been elevated as such in many of my work endeavors.

While honored by the experience, this elevation to leadership has also proven to be a target and area of possible insecurity amongst others that I have worked with. As I grew in leadership, I realized how threatened some professionals were with my presence and ability to excel.

I learned very quickly that if I didn't speak up for myself and define what I needed and wanted within my career trajectory, this idea that others would do so on my behalf was non-existent.

My professional background was not an area that I could just hope for the best in. I had to make it the best through action and delivery.

This meant that I couldn't play the role of the sheep and blend into the back and let others talk over me, disregard my thoughts, or steal my ideas without objection. I had to learn to stand strong, to document instances of unprofessionalism, and to address them with tact.

Sometimes actions were taken out of a pure unawareness of their possible repercussions to myself and others.

Other times, I found that certain actions were taken deliberately and sometimes out of malice.

Either way, my approach to lessening the instance had to come from a place of pure intention and an opportunity to teach and connect with the professional(s) at hand on a deeper level.

This is another example of a challenge in my life that helped to groom me in many other areas.

As I began to learn my worth and walk in my value, I realized that while I could not change the hearts of everyone around me, I did have to lead others in seeing that the respect I carried within myself and for myself, was something that I also required from the outside world. An absence of respect on a continual basis meant that I was in an environment that was not meant for me.

Sometimes we think that turning a blind eye to disrespect and being the 'bigger person' is the way to go; However, the more we allow others to impede on our progress, peace of mind and respect of self, the easier it is for us to invite a continued cycle of disregard within our lives.

This doesn't mean that you should fight every battle or go tit for tat on every insult that comes your way. Keep in mind that what you conceive as an insult may not be done in ill intention. Making others aware of areas of concern around their actions and said actions impact on your circumstances, offers an area of opportunity to lessen stress and continued ill will.

Not only that, it offers an opportunity for teaching, collaboration and a deeper understanding of each party's stance and point of view.

We all come from different backgrounds, mindsets and ideas. Directly approaching areas of concern with compassion is most necessary in offering an ability to connect with others on a deeper level.

As you begin to move in peace, assume positive intent from others until they prove otherwise.

Defining what you will accept reaches further than just what we consider when it comes to romantic relationships. Defining what you will accept has to be something that we are comfortable doing in friendships, family matters and professional settings as well.

Defining and living by what you will accept allows you to operate with a greater sense of control over your outcomes as well as a clearer awareness of environments and relationships that no longer benefit you.

Say no to begging for what you deserve or accepting less than what is appropriate.

Be aware of your wants and needs.

Walk in a respectful manner.

Assume positive intent and address boundaries that are crossed with tact and understanding.

As they are revealed, begin to turn a blind eye to any and every environment that is not willing to treat you with the respect that you so rightfully deserve. Remove yourself from it and act as if it does not exist.

Drawing boundaries and living in environments of respect are imperative aspects to your continued peace of mind.

13.

HEALTH IS WEALTH

Rodney couldn't believe the day's turn.

As he laid sprawled out on his front lawn, heart racing, he gripped his chest and tried hard just to breath.

This can't be life...

He thought to himself as he listened to his frantic wife call for an ambulance.

Please, 'come quick...it's my husband'.

The sky seemed to start spinning and then faded to a blur.

Rodney lost consciousness.

The numbing pain in Rodney's left arm had been a painful reminder for the past several weeks, urging him to book a doctor's appointment. But with all of the competing interests in life, he kept thinking, I'll do it tomorrow...

All too suddenly, tomorrow was here and despite his plans for the day, he found himself looking up from some hospital bed to stained, off-white colored ceiling tiles and a sheer, ugly, beige curtain blocking him from the other patients he was now sharing a space with.

His senses filled with the stench of sterilization, blood and sickness. All that he could think of was how badly he wanted to go home.

Now.

His wife's voice broke his thoughts of disgust as she appeared at the foot of his hospital bed.

'Sweetheart....you're okay! The doctors say you're okay. They're just running some tests to see what happened. They think you might have had a stroke...'

Her words faded as Rodney held back tears and a knot in his throat that seemed to appear without notice.

Frustration filled his veins.

As tired as he was, all that he felt inside was anger.

Without warning, he began to flashback to memories of his childhood. He heard the screams of his father filling his ears as if he had been transported back in time…

“Get up!”

“Get the fuck up right now!”

“You weak. You weak little boy, I won’t stand for it! No son of mine is going to walk around like some bum. Stand the fuck up, NOW!”

Rodney’s eight year old self stood up, quickly and with pride. He poked his chest out and held back his tears just as he had been taught to do for years now. He knew he had taken exactly the stance his father was looking for yet still, he saw his fathers oversized shoe headed for his tiny face.

He remembered falling back into the floor and bursting into tears.

His father was a difficult man. Never much satisfied with Rodney, his mother, or his brothers and sisters. But Rodney got the brunt of it. As his father’s oldest son, he was an example to everyone to keep quiet, act right and do whatever his father said to do, when he said do it, without question.

Rodney lived in a state of stress and fear for much of his childhood.

Still, he grew to be a responsible and caring man.

He married, had three children of his own, his youngest graduating from high school in just a few weeks.

Rodney only saw his past in his dreams but as he sat in this hospital bed, all that he could hear, see and feel were his father....

While his trauma had left his mind, it seemed it had not at all left his body and innermost being.

The streets, a scared mother and a controlling and hostile father raised Rodney.

Now at the age of fifty-six, with a beautiful tribe of his own raised with all the care and compassion that he could offer, he realized just how relevant his past still was to him.

Rodney was tired.

Physically and mentally, tired.

He was always ripping and running to provide for his family and keep everyone happy and healthy that he had little to no time to offer himself the same.

Rodney barely ever discussed his past with his wife or children. He shared a few intimate stories with his wife but always held the stance that he'd shelter his children from those memories. That's just the way that it was back in the day and his aim was to instead share with them hope and the beauty that tomorrow could bring. A mindset that he was not afforded as a child.

Despite this lack of acknowledgement, his trauma was still apparent in his inability to sleep, his binge eating and his consistent need to overwork and stay busy to provide for and satisfy his families needs.

Rodney never took vacations or cared for himself. Of no fault or ill intention, it was an afterthought to his family as well. For all of their lives they had watched their father take care of home and his responsibilities as second nature. It always seemed to come so easy to him. They never saw him weak or frazzled. He always knew what to do next and just did it.

He was the hero of the whole family.

But seeing Rodney lying in the hospital bed, a first for both his wife and children, bought flooding realizations to the whole family.

Their reality sat in the hospital bed looking back at them.

We've got to take better care of dad…

So many of our families have experienced a similar story to Rodney's…

Not thinking about health and the impact of past trauma and lifestyles until we're made to through tragedy or pain.

As we begin to deepen the self love that we have for ourselves and that we provide to our families and friends, the health of our physical being must be at the forefront of that planning.

A weak foundation tumbles.

Our temple needs to have the endurance and longevity to carry out what our strong minds and spirits cannot do alone. We must hold a respect for our temples at the forefront of our growth and development. We cannot reach our full potential in one realm if we disregard another.

We are a generation of people who have internalized trauma from our ancestors, parents, grandparents and the weight of the societal structure that we are exposed to.

Whether we acknowledge or even believe in the weight of generational trauma, it impacts us. Those of us who grew up privileged or poor; on the 'good side of town' or the bad; with J's, chuck taylors or payless knockoffs. The impact of generational trauma in America does not pick and choose its victims.

It impacts all of us, collectively, in some way or another.

To continue to feed our bodies with substances that do nothing to replenish, yet everything to break us down, makes us a detriment to ourselves.

Despite what many are willing to say, we are poisoning ourselves with the ways that we feed and care for our bodies.

It has to stop.

We cannot grow as a people if we are weighed down not only by our trauma, but by our additions to pacifying that trauma with what we eat, drink and how we engage with one another.

We cannot grow as a people if we cannot defend ourselves and fight back, both physically and mentally against transgressions aimed at us. And we cannot grow as a people if we are dependent upon poison to fuel our bodies more often than we replenish our beings with nutrients.

The body is no different than the mind. If we feed it enough negativity, that negativity will have the most impact.

We are weighing our physical bodies down with as much trauma as our spiritual and mental beings have been exposed to and this is something we just can't afford.

More often than not, we are not concerned with our health or our families health, until someone is lying in a hospital bed, like Rodney. Where we then find ourselves perplexed at how life took such a turn but not acknowledging that we were building a foundation to that very fate, all along.

As a community of people struggling from generational trauma and our own personal experiences with trauma, our bodies hold on to a level of stress that in and of itself attracts hardship, disease and discomfort.

We have to be intentional in tending to that stress with consistent efforts and change.

We cannot continue to grow accustomed to hardships that we are meant to rise above.

This world is going to make it easier for us to poison ourselves than to heal.

That is why we must be intentional and aware of the attacks against our very being that takes place inadvertently, every day.

Self respect and self love means feeding your body what it needs to thrive.

Raising your energy levels and vibrational energy are more than just meditation and prayer. It is an all encompassing act of providing yourself with proper nutrition and movement to allow your mind and spirit to reach its highest potential.

This doesn't mean perfection.

It doesn't mean that you can never eat a burger from a fast food joint.

But it does mean that you become conscientious and responsible for the health and wellbeing of your temple.

This is a layer of discipline and self love that will wholeheartedly change the game for you and your family.

Small but simple steps in providing yourself with better nutrition and lifestyle habits will allow you to lay the most sturdy foundation of love that will not crumble with ease but instead bear the weight of this world on top of it.

Spiritual and mental healing will never be complete without an emphasis on physical well being.

We cannot build upon what is too easy to tear down. The efforts start within.

19.

WALKING IN TRUTH

Tempers were running high.

You could literally feel the heat in the atmosphere as protesters stood outside the capital.

After years of continued police brutality, an unresolved pandemic and both personal and economic uncertainty, US citizens had had enough.

Bryce could feel the tension in the air and felt anxious as he stood in the crowd with a group of his friends.

While he felt moved by the state of injustice he was living in and witnessing first hand, a part of him wasn't sure that he was meant to be a part of the chaos that was unfolding right before his eyes.

On one end he desired to fight for what was right. A close friend of his had experienced the injustices of police brutality first hand and several members of his family were victims of mass incarceration and its effects.

Bryce grew up listening to stories of uncles and aunts who weren't able to vote, receive consistent employment and had questions of their own self worth and value after being locked up for long periods of time.

Now, in an era where many of the crimes they were previously locked up for were being decriminalized, and widely accepted amongst Americans, he shared in the frustrations of family members who now felt that their years of suffering were all in vain.

On the other end, Bryce was young, only twenty years old, he couldn't even legally drink, yet was socially pulled by his peers to stand up for and fight against the hatred of white supremacy, the injustices of police brutality and the unjust foundation of capitalism in America that targeted black and brown men and women while elevating and providing unfair privilege to white Americans.

It all seemed so overwhelming.

At one point he found himself asking his group of friends,

'wait we're fighting for all of this at the capitol in one day?'

He jokingly laughed to keep it light hearted but really wanted to fish for a reasonable answer.

Standing in solidarity with his peers was something that he would partake in on any given day and he did so with both dignity and pride.

But the chaos that was unfolding before him was a reflection of hatred, disgust and rage.

There were no voices of reason.

Those that stood for reason were overwhelmingly silenced by those filled with rage.

All that Bryce saw before him was pent up frustration, alcohol induced speech and violence and young people choosing to engage in an attack upon their very own government instead of reasonable steps and actions towards positive change.

Deep down in his consciousness, Bryce did not feel that he was meant to be a part of this movement, on this day. It seemed like one group against another in an environment filled with chaos.

He had felt a strong pull in his spirit before even making the drive to DC.

The risks seemed to outweigh the benefits and he was uncertain around how the evening and days actions would ultimately unfold.

Bryce was encompassed by a feeling he was too prideful to admit.

A feeling that was grounded in fear.

We are living in a time where standing up for a worthy cause is both memorable and adventurous.

Protests have always been amongst the fabric of American culture and are still widely accepted and glorified due to the many needs for justice and political change that many citizens acknowledge and agree upon.

It is honorable to be living in a time of true American history and being a part of *writing that history* through individual engagement is liberating.

As many young people become more active in standing up for what they believe is right, it is important to acknowledge that while many of the efforts that we see are grounded in a pure desire for justice behind worthy causes, there are also just as many opportunists using these moments for their own personal gain or social initiatives.

What you must consider in this environment is whether or not you are a sheep amongst wolves, or standing planted in your own state of truth.

It is easy to be swayed into action, especially when it seems to be of popular belief.

It is important to take into account that media outlets and sources of power have always had a way of highlighting and swaying the minds of viewers for initiatives and reasons that we may not totally comprehend.

When you decide to take part in a risk, ensure that it is a worthy cause to you, the individual.

You need not consider your family, social group, educational background, race, creed, color or gender as a sole worthy cause to risk your life or well being. What you stand for must be true to you in your heart of hearts and not something that you are simply convinced to do.

Many people are wearing the face of a supporter or ally without holding the heart of one.

To risk your life, well-being or character, in any environment - for another man's cause, is an unnecessary act and state of being. It is an action that screams of self validation and fitting in, instead of an acknowledgement of your own truths, research and understanding.

Understanding, evaluating and weighing the risks of your actions and beliefs is a part of deeply rooting yourself in your own value system, instead of just joining or involving yourself in that of what you see.

Just because a million people take part in an act or say they stand for a cause does not mean that their words or actions are bred in truth.

Protests are just one relevant example in today's time. They are neither right nor wrong at large, but something every individual must decide whether to embark in for themselves. There are many avenues for change and societal influence, and you must choose to involve yourself in what makes sense for you.

The consequences of your choices will not weigh heavily on anyone but yourself. Make sure that for every action that you take, you are willing to bear the brunt of its consequences, whether they fall in your favor or not.

Everything in this life that you do should be a reflection of the inner you:

Your value system, your beliefs, your fun, your adventures and your desires.

Legacy building will have everything to do with your own experiences, moral standings and actions. The world around us will continue to evolve and take many different shapes and forms. We can be molded by it or consider and acknowledge our own unique footprints and have an influence that shapes others instead of solely being shaped ourselves.

To lead in a world of followers is admirable.

To choose risks that are not grounded in our own truth could turn to watered down regrets with impacts that we are not able to turn from.

Choose your risks wisely. Shape the world around you with your own powerful influence.

Walking in your own unique truth is the only action that comes with no regret.

When walking within your own value system -
even when you lose, you learn.

15.

IT'S HARD TO SAY GOODBYE

Savannah had had her share of eligible bachelors.

From wealthy, to cool, to slick, to in shape - she had seen it all and turned down her fair share of handsome and successful men.

But somehow, meeting Miguel was like a dream she couldn't wake up from.

From the moment she laid eyes on him she was captivated and drawn into something deeper than she could fathom. She daydreamed with the thought but only for a moment, letting it pass with the sun of that day.

Miguel didn't come with any flashing lights or smoke alarms drawing attention to the fact that he was the one. He just…came.

Appeared within Savannah's life and captured her soul upon arrival.

He was charming, sure. But a charm that Savannah could tell had been sharpened with time and was placed in each moment and circumstance with careful consideration and thought.

In the beginning, she totally ignored it.

Miguel seemed to be a player. There was so much mystery behind him. He was quiet but forthcoming. Sly while also being direct. There was just something about him that gave her reservation....

She tried her best to ignore his advances and remain focused on her own life and more realistic romantic possibilities.

Still somehow, on a random night, at an event full of admirers, she found herself lost in the thought of him. Wanting to explore something that she had never expressed to him or even herself.

Several weeks later, their intimacy began to unfold.

First, mentally.

Then, physically...

His touch sent shivers down her spine. Scared to explore they stumbled upon each other's sexuality with an awkwardness that only they could understand. A glance, a touch, a joke and then an awareness that this moment was theirs to share.

Too afraid to look each other in the eyes, they shared passionate kisses and touches that bought out a softness in Savannah that she had never experienced.

In his arms, she seemed to be another woman.

Warm, silky, awakened and free.

Their intimacy went deeper than the touch.

It was like he breathed into her soul and took over.

She couldn't shake him.

Soon after their first encounter, her world began to change.

A day without Miguel felt like the edge of death. Savannah felt overwhelmed and as if she couldn't breath, think or focus, unless it was within the presence of his love. She enjoyed their connection and allowed herself to get lost in the passion of each moment.

Their infatuation with each other lasted for months. And then one day, without warning, Savannah woke up, and there was no more Miguel.

Her phone calls went unanswered.

Visits they planned in advance never occurred.

Out of nowhere, Miguel was out of sight, touch and communication and seemed to want nothing more to do with Savannah.

Savannah dwelled on this loss for some time.

When Miguel shared his affection, his time and his conversation, Savannah was above herself. She was the woman that she always wanted to be. She didn't care about a thing and could get lost in her ideas of herself and her sweet Miguel.

When he took himself away, she felt less than a portion of herself.

Lost, devastated, obsessive and empty. A woman that she had never seen before. And not just for a moment. Savannah found herself spending days submersed in this emptiness and pain.

Days lost in a desire for his presence, for his love, for his voice and for his touch. She felt spiritually starved without him and though she'd try to rise above it, the more pain he provided, the deeper his trance and the more fixated on the thought of him she became.

It was like he had eaten her soul and left her with only the bones and a partially beating heart.

Several weeks passed and Savannah's sadness deepened. Miguel was wrong for leaving her so suddenly, with no warning or reason. Yet still in her heart of hearts, she still felt that she loved him.

Despite her deepest reasoning, she wanted nothing more than just an opportunity to see his face again.

I experienced an infatuation like this before.

It was strong.

I loved him.

At least - I thought I did.

Feelings that ran deeper than a well. Shaking them felt impossible.

I always wondered why the 'bad boys' - unpredictable, fleeting, unavailable and cold men were able to captivate so much of my attention. I'd never been boy crazy. I enjoy romancing and being in a relationship but I equally enjoy my time to myself and seasons in solitude.

So I never had many lovers.

Yet there were seasons of my life, where I fell for and wasted time with men that I knew weren't good for me. Typically, I'd come to a realization, bear with my feelings, and let it go.

Falling for this particular man however, proved different. Not only was it difficult for me to walk away, I grieved for the loss much longer than I anticipated.

I fought it.

I tried to bring the cards of his heart back into my hands. I pleaded, I prodded, I negotiated…

In my spirit, I felt that he was mine and I was his, and his words and actions that proved different were only a ploy.

I couldn't let go.

Saying goodbye is never easy. Whether it be to a friend, lover, family member or even business relationship. That five year employment, decade old marriage that turns to divorce or even the short fling that just bought us the hope of something more - they all feel the same.

We get so used to what works for us and so tied up in our dreams, that making a change that requires a loss of what is familiar can be very unwelcoming.

I still struggle with feelings of anxiety, especially in these moments.

Moments where I've made up in my mind that something or someone was for me and would never not be for me.

But the only constant in life is uncertainty and change.

They come knocking at your doorstep when you least expect it and you must accept them whether you agree to, or not.

As I began to grow in my understanding and ideas of self worth, I realized that most of these relationships and instances that I held onto were not because they were truly beneficial or nurturing to me, but instead - familiar connections.

Connections that linked me to my wounded inner child. Deep down, my inner being had seen a resemblance in these relationships to the pain of my past. I frantically held on to the relationship in the hopes that this time around, I could transform it to what it was *supposed to be.*

How they were supposed to love me.

How I was supposed to feel and share my love.

How I could change their mind if just given the chance...

But the 'love' was never actually love.

Cold, distant, untruthful and unfulfilling - it was a representation of my past and the 'me' that still held onto the hope that I was valuable enough to *be loved.*

The problem was not that I was not valuable, but I was seeking validation from sources that were not equipped to offer that love to begin with.

The more hurtful, unwelcome and disruptive the relationship grew, the deeper I became drawn into my obsession with proving myself worthy.

It was a very sad chapter in my life but something that I had to first accept and understand to change.

From a young age, dysfunction and abandonment were inserted into my life like a drug. As an adult I didn't realize the ways in which I continued to welcome it. But life's path somehow always led me to it.

I inhaled and filled myself up with the emptiness that each encounter offered and when it was finally all gone, I'd wait for the next hit of familiarity to become lost in.

All of my relationships were not as equally toxic and many offered me companionship and compassion in some form or another, but many also had lingerings of the pain that I continued to relate to and attract to my life.

If there was nothing to fix or no one to prove my value to, it was not a relationship that I wholeheartedly pursued.

Some people have shared concern with me that I have taken away the responsibility of the abuser in speaking in this manner.

The problem at hand is not that every encounter was per-say abusive within my realm. Some were just not fulfilling and right *for me*. When I began to fill myself up with love, to understand what kind of love that I needed to flourish, to be replenished and to move forward with fruitful relationships, that's when my life changed.

So it's not so much that I have ever made excuses for the behaviors of abusers, as much as I have rather chosen to empower and embody a woman that does not invite abusive tendencies into her life.

This is where I found the greatest source of all of my power. The greatest source of understanding and healing.

This is what led me to true love.

While saying goodbye in those moments, the broken Nicole felt - lost, depleted and depressed.

But saying goodbye in those moments as the whole and healed and worth Nicole felt - empowering and awakening and true.

I began to move forward in life knowing that what God had in store for me was so much more beautiful than I had ever imagined.

However hurtful, unwelcome or disruptive change may be, we must learn to welcome it.

We must seek the wisdom and knowledge of what is most purposeful for our journey as healed men and women and courageously walk away from what lies outside of that.

Especially as we seek growth.

In these moments, I encourage you to let go.

Replace your desire to fight the transformation and learn to love it and to be patient with what is taking place.

Replace your fear with faith.

A faith that all that you have grown to be and repair will work in your favor.

A faith that the love and relationships that you desire will find their way to you, and stay.

A faith that the success that you yearn for, you are on the right path to receive.

A faith that the seeds that you have planted will bloom and all that it will take is time and the proper watering.

When life places you in a position to say goodbye, welcome that goodbye with the faith that a new hello will fulfill your spirit with healing, replenishment and a love that is right for you.

16.
THE PATH TO PURPOSE

Writing my first book, Uncovering Your Power, was easy.

It was easy because it was a book written from true passion, emotion and a strong desire to make available for others what I couldn't find for myself during a pivotal aspect of my journey.

Compassion, understanding and guidance.

Promoting Uncovering Your Power to the outside world, however, was more difficult.

I had so many ideas and was moved by so many aspects of offering healing to others who struggled with domestic violence that I thought it would be easy. As I began to realize my plans to turn my journals into a book, there seemed to be nothing that could put out the fire of passion burning within me.

Speaking to the issues of abuse didn't come with such ease.

It came with difficulty because domestic violence, childhood abuse, speaking to someone you know is a victim or initiator of abuse, and the like - are not topics that many people feel comfortable speaking openly about or addressing head on.

Yes, many consider the idea a worthy cause. Many will watch movies or documentaries at their own will about abuse and the harms of it. Yes, it is a realistic part of our societal makeup.

But still, it is not what many would perceive or dive into as a *popular* topic of interest.

It also came with difficulty because of my own experiences and the fact that my testimony affected real people who had their own opinions of truth and the next course of action that I should or should not have taken in my life.

There have been many times in life where I found my thinking and processing of information out of line with the majority. Because of this, I have often felt misunderstood.

I spent a lot of past energy trying to get others to agree with or understand my stance instead of simply walking in it.

I realized very quickly after finalizing my book that this was a project that I would have to have the strength to build alone and to brace myself for the conflicting thoughts, ideas and values that would present themselves in the process.

I had to dedicate myself to walking in the direction that my spirit led me, no matter what.

There were many times that I second guessed myself and my actions.

> *Should I promote to this audience?*
>
> *Should I tell my inner circle, colleagues and associates what this book is really about?*
>
> *Should I expose myself?*
>
> *Should I speak to what I learned from my past or just let it go because it's over with?*

Doubt creeped into so many aspects of this journey and there were more than a few times that I thought to myself, to hell with this...

Allowing myself to possibly be defined as a woman who had suffered at the hands of abuse was scary to me. I knew how strong and worthy I was of true love and I did not want to taint my worth with such vulnerability. I struggled with this internally.

There came a time where I had to acknowledge my fear and make a choice:

Would I feed my ego or my purpose?

My *ego* wanted to show the world how strong I was. How much of a leader I was and highlight my ability to conquer any battle. My *ego* did not want to be limited to this one story that some might perceive as defeat, amongst the many other successful adventures within my life.

My *passion* wanted to create a path for others. To share compassion and support in an area and around a topic that is often overlooked. My *passion* was to help victims uncover a path to greater peace within their lives.

My *ego* led me to questioning myself and doubts and a lack of action because of the possible response.

My *passion* led me to prayers on my knees to God and my ancestors, often.

My *ego* led to wasted time trying to win over doubters by speaking out against statements meant to induce shame and a second look at myself.

My *passion* would help to heal souls.

My *ego* would only lead to a satisfaction of self…

My *passion* would be an example of what was possible to all.

My greatest take away from this internal dialog was to follow my spirit which ultimately revealed to me my purpose.

In the midst of writing Uncovering, I did not wake up one day and realize that I was fulfilling my purpose. I just simply did what was on my heart. But after opening myself up and allowing myself to be moved by passion and spirituality, and a closed door to my ego, my purpose revealed itself.

When you feel moved or deeply inspired, consider it the rumbling of purpose within your life. Act upon it. Whether it's popular, in demand or seems out of this world crazy... don't be afraid to act upon it.

Allow yourself to define yourself within your own realm, whether others understand it or not.

The creator works in mysterious ways. What you may think is just something you did out of the blue, could be laying the framework for something great that only you are meant to accomplish.

There is only one you and only you can perform the acts of God that are intended for you.

Have an open heart and act upon your passions with faith.

Either you're going to find your purpose or your purpose is going to find you.

Either way, you win.

To serve your life's purpose is to elevate society as a whole...

"Our deepest fear is not that we are inadequate. Our deepest fear is that we are powerful beyond measure. It is our light, not our darkness, that most frightens us.

We ask ourselves: Who am I to be brilliant,gorgeous, talented, and fabulous?

Who are you not to be?

Your playing small does not serve the world.

There is nothing enlightened about shrinking, so that others won't feel insecure around you. We were born to make manifest the glory of God that is within us.

It's not just in some of us: it's in everyone.

And, as we let our own light shine, we unconsciously give other people permission to do the same. As we are liberated from our fear, our presence automatically liberates others..."

Nelson Mandela,
1993 Inauguration Speech

Made in the USA
Middletown, DE
10 January 2022